Chorale Partitas

KOMT NU MET ZANG, MOZART, PUER NOBIS

by
Robert LeBlanc

LITURGICAL PRESS
Collegeville, Minnesota

www.litpress.org

ACKNOWLEDGMENTS

Cover design: Monica Bokinskie.

ISBN: 978-0-8146-6373-8

Preface

Variation technique is at the heart of any composer's craft. It is also the bread and butter of any practicing organist, for whom improvisation is an indispensable skill. Of course, this skill extends well beyond simply filling "empty space" in the liturgical action, rather it encompasses everything from teaching new congregational hymn tunes to playing preludes and postludes, "setting the mood" liturgically, as well as interpreting selected hymns through creative harmonizations, textures, registration, tempi, and rhythm. Careful use of these elements is the means by which we minister to the church at prayer Sunday after Sunday.

For those, however, who find improvisation difficult or are otherwise unfamiliar or uneasy in its practice, I offer these variations for your use in any way that serves your ministry. Several of the movements may be used as short preludes to introduce the tunes, while others may even be appropriate as accompaniments or used *ad alternatim* with congregational singing. It is important to note that the individual variations need not be played in sequence as written here—though I feel they serve well as a set.

For those who wish to grow as improvisers, perhaps these variations will spark your own creativity. I urge you to explore the vast repertoire of organ literature and learn from the many generations of organists who preceded our own.

Robert LeBlanc

I. Chorale Partita on "What Is This Place"

KOMT NU MET ZANG

Robert LeBlanc

I.

II.

Tune: KOMT NU MET ZANG, 9 8 9 8 9 66; Valerius' *Neder-landtsche gedenck-klanck.*
Music: *Chorale Partitas,* © 2019, Robert LeBlanc, b. 1948. Published and administered by Liturgical Press, Collegeville, MN 56321.

III.
1.
2.
IV.
1.
2.

*May be played an octave higher at 4' pitch.

VII.
I.
II.
VIII.
I.
II.

slowly and lyrically
IX.
I. (gentle reed 8')
1.
II. (flute 8')
ped. (gedeckt 8')
2.
II.
I.
molto rit.
a tempo
rit.

* May be played without pedal on one or two manuals.
** Thumb down from top manual if played without pedal.

II. Chorale Partita on "Your Hands, O Lord, in Days of Old"

MOZART

Robert LeBlanc

Tune: MOZART, 86 86 D; adapt. from Wolfgang A. Mozart, 1756-1791.

III.
man.

IV.
flexibly
3
3
3
3
1
2
V.
I.
II.

II.
I.
VI.
I.
II.

I.
II.

VII.
II.
I.
ped.

For Bruce Bengtson
in friendship

III. Chorale Partita on "That Easter Day with Joy Was Bright"

PUER NOBIS

Robert LeBlanc

* *May be played an octave higher (at 4' pitch).*

Tune: PUER NOBIS, 88 88; Michael Praetorius, 1571-1621, adapt.

III.
L.H.
calmly
IV.
I.
II.

V.
VI.
I.
II.

* *This various should be played up an octave on a 16' manual stop to accommodate the low 'B' in the penultimate measure.*

* *Small note to be played only if no 16' stop available. See suggestion on preceding page.*